This book was compiled by Daniel Melehi
with the A.I assistance of Inventabot

Dedication

I hope this helps all of my wonderful
readers achieve all their goals in their
business. And I would like to thank my
wonderful wife for all of her continued
support in all my ventures.

May 7 2023

Contents

Chapter 1: Introduction to Custom Add-Ons for Magento Magento is a powerful and flexible e-commerce platform, well-known for its extensive feature set and ability to support large-scale online stores. However, even though Magento comes with a rich set of features out-of-the-box, there are still cases where companies would like to have a custom functionality. This is where custom add-ons come into play, as they can provide additional functionality to the existing Magento installation, allowing businesses to tailor their e-commerce store to their specific needs. In this book, "Raking In Revenue with Custom Add-Ons for Magento", we will explore the world of custom add-ons for Magento, their benefits, and how to plan and create them. We will also discuss how to implement custom add-ons, market and sell them, and provide maintenance and support. Finally, we will take a closer look at some case studies and future developments in the field. So, let's dive right in and discover the exciting world of Magento custom add-ons!

Introduction to Custom Add-Ons for Magento

Magento is one of the most powerful and flexible e-commerce platforms available today. However, to truly maximize its potential, businesses may need to utilize custom add-ons. These add-ons can add essential features, improve performance, and enhance the user experience on your Magento site.

UNDERSTANDING MAGENTO'S ARCHITECTURE

Before diving into custom add-ons, it's important to first understand Magento's architecture. Magento is built on the Model-View-Controller (MVC) design pattern, which separates the different components of a web application into distinct layers. At its core, Magento consists of a set of PHP files that handle requests and produce responses. These files are organized into modules, which can be thought of as self-contained units of functionality.

BENEFITS OF CUSTOM ADD-ONS

There are many benefits to utilizing custom add-ons on your Magento site. Some of the key advantages include:

- Adding new features
- Improving performance
- Enhancing user experience
- Increasing sales and revenue
- Improving search engine optimization (SEO)

Custom add-ons can help businesses to differentiate themselves from their competitors and offer unique value to their customers. In the next chapter, we'll explore how to plan and create custom add-ons to achieve these benefits.

UNDERSTANDING MAGENTO'S ARCHITECTURE

Magento is a powerful and versatile e-commerce platform that boasts a complex architecture, which makes it one of the most flexible and customizable shopping carts. In this subchapter, we will delve into the concepts and principles that underlie Magento's architecture. At its core, Magento is built with a modular architecture based on the Model-View-Controller (MVC) design pattern. This means that the application logic, user interface, and data model are separated into distinct components that interact with each other through well-defined interfaces. From a technical standpoint, the Magento architecture is composed of the following layers:

Frontend Layer

This layer includes all the customer-facing components such as the homepage, category pages, product pages, shopping cart, and checkout. The frontend layer is responsible for rendering the HTML and CSS of the web pages and handling user input and interactions.

Backend Layer

The backend layer includes all the administrative components such as the admin panel, product management, order management, and customer management. The backend layer is responsible for managing the underlying data model and business logic.

Integration Layer

The integration layer is responsible for connecting Magento with third-party systems such as payment processors, shipping providers, and CRM software. This layer uses APIs and web services to communicate with external systems and exchange data.

Infrastructure Layer

The infrastructure layer includes the hosting environment, web servers, and database servers. This layer is responsible for providing the resources and services required to run the Magento application. Understanding the different layers of Magento's architecture is essential for developing custom add-ons that integrate seamlessly with the platform. In the next subchapter, we will explore the benefits of custom add-ons and how they can help you improve your e-commerce business.

BENEFITS OF CUSTOM ADD-ONS

Custom add-ons offer numerous benefits for Magento store owners, providing unique functionalities and improving the user experience for their customers. Here are some of the benefits of custom add-ons:

1. Tailor-made solutions

Custom add-ons allow store owners to create tailor-made solutions that cater to their unique business needs. They can create features and functionalities that are not available in the default Magento platform, giving them a competitive edge in their industry.

2. Improved customer experience

Custom add-ons can help improve the customer's shopping experience by providing additional features that make it easier for them to find what they are looking for. This can include personalized recommendations, advanced search functionalities, and improved checkout processes.

3. Increased revenue

Custom add-ons can help increase revenue for store owners by offering unique functionalities and features that can differentiate their store from their competitors. This can help attract more customers and lead to increased sales and profits.

4. Scalability and flexibility

Custom add-ons allow store owners to create scalable and flexible solutions that can adapt to their changing business needs. As their business grows, they can easily add new functionalities and features to their store without having to completely rebuild their website. Overall, custom add-ons are a valuable investment for any Magento store owner looking to improve their store's functionalities, improve the user experience, and increase revenue.

Chapter 2: Planning and Creating Custom Add-Ons

SUBCHAPTER 2.1: IDENTIFYING BUSINESS NEEDS

To create an effective custom add-on for your Magento store, you first need to identify your business needs. This means asking the right questions and pinpointing exactly what you hope to achieve with your add-on. Some questions to consider include: - What specific functionality are you looking to add to your store? - What pain points do your customers experience when using your site? - Are there any features missing from Magento that you'd like to see? - How can you improve the user experience on your site? - Are there any third-party integrations you need for your business operations? By clearly defining your business needs, you can create a roadmap for your custom add-on development that addresses those needs.

SUBCHAPTER 2.2: CREATING A DEVELOPMENT PLAN

Once you've identified your business needs, the next step is to create a development plan for your custom add-on. Your plan should include a timeline for development, budget considerations, resource allocation, and project milestones. It's important to ensure that your development plan is both realistic and achievable. This means clearly outlining the steps involved in the development process and ensuring that you have the necessary resources in place (such as skilled developers, project managers, and testing tools). Your development plan should also include a thorough testing and quality assurance process to ensure that your custom add-on is ready to go live.

SUBCHAPTER 2.3: MAGENTO DEVELOPMENT BEST PRACTICES

To create a successful custom add-on for Magento, you'll need to follow best practices for development. These include: - Adhering to the Magento coding standards to ensure that your code is maintainable and scalable - Implementing efficient database schema and structure - Using extensions and plug-ins that are compatible with the latest version of Magento - Following proper testing and debugging procedures to ensure that your add-on works smoothly - Utilizing version control systems to make it easier to track changes and roll back to a previous version if necessary By following these best practices, you can ensure that your custom add-on integrates seamlessly with Magento and provides a reliable and effective solution for your business needs.

IDENTIFYING BUSINESS NEEDS

Before creating custom add-ons for Magento, it is crucial to identify the specific business needs that the add-on will address. This involves analyzing the current state of the business processes and determining areas where customizations can optimize workflow and increase revenue. One effective strategy is to conduct surveys and interviews with stakeholders to gain a thorough understanding of the daily challenges and pain points faced in the day-to-day aspects of running the business. This information can then be used to identify and prioritize requirements for custom add-ons. It is important to ensure that the identified needs align with the overall business goals and customer needs. This will ensure that the add-on not only enhances internal processes but also adds value to the customer experience. By taking the time to identify business needs, the resulting custom add-on will be more effective and provide a higher return on investment.

CREATING A DEVELOPMENT PLAN

Creating a development plan is an essential step in the process of building custom add-ons for Magento. A well-planned development process aids in delivering the project within the stipulated time frame, within budget, and of high quality. Here are some key components of a successful development plan:

Set Clear Objectives and Goals

The first step in creating a development plan is setting clear project objectives and goals. These objectives and goals should be specific, measurable, achievable, relevant, and time-bound (SMART). Defining SMART goals and objectives help to stay focused, measure progress, and make relevant changes to the development plan along the way.

Develop an Implementation Strategy

Once the project objectives are set, the next step is to develop a strategy for implementation. The implementation strategy should include project timelines, resource allocation, and deliverables. All team members should know what is expected of them, their deadlines, and the reporting procedures.

Determine the Requirements

Once the objectives and implementation strategy are in place, the next step is to determine the requirements for custom add-ons. This includes understanding the customer needs, gathering requirements, prioritizing them, and defining them in detail.

Create a Project Plan and Schedule

With the requirements in hand, the next step is to create a project plan and schedule. This includes a breakdown of tasks, timelines, and dependencies. A well-defined plan and schedule help to ensure that the tasks are completed on schedule and within budget.

Establish a Communication Plan

Communication is key in project development. Establishing a communication plan ensures that all team members are informed about the project progress, issues, and next steps. This includes regular team meetings, progress reports, and project updates. Creating a development plan helps to ensure a successful outcome for custom add-ons for Magento. A well-planned development process not only helps to stay on track but also aids in delivering the project of high quality and within budget.

MAGENTO DEVELOPMENT BEST PRACTICES

Magento is a highly customizable e-commerce platform that can accommodate various business requirements with its customizable features. However, developing custom add-ons for Magento requires some best practices to ensure the add-on is reliable and secure. In this section, we'll discuss some key Magento development best practices that will help you create custom add-ons for Magento effectively.

Coding Standards

Following coding standards helps ensure the code is maintainable and consistent. Magento has defined coding standards, which developers should follow when designing custom add-ons for Magento. Adhering to these standards improves the overall code quality and reduces the chances of errors.

Data Security

Since Magento stores sensitive customer data, data security is vital while developing custom add-ons. Developers should use secure coding practices and adopt Magento's security features while building custom add-ons. It includes practices like using prepared statements for queries, sanitizing user input, and more.

Scalability

Magento stores can expect rapid growth, so scalability is another key consideration in developing custom add-ons for Magento. Developers must ensure that custom add-ons don't significantly affect site performance. Optimizing queries, caching, and load balancing are essential considerations for scalability.

Testing

Testing is vital to ensure that custom add-ons function as expected and don't cause issues when integrated with Magento.

Developers should write unit tests for custom add-ons that test specific functionalities and integration tests to ensure a smooth integration with Magento.

Documentation

Documenting custom add-ons help developers understand the code, making it easier to maintain and make updates as well as making the integration of the custom add-ons seamless. It also improves future upgrades and helps resolve any issues quickly. Some recommended documents detail the custom add-ons' functionalities, developer notes, and any known compatibility or security risks. Adopting these best practices while developing custom add-ons for Magento ensures custom add-ons' reliability, scalability, and security and provide a great user experience for the merchants' end-users.

Chapter 3: Implementing Custom Add-Ons

SUBCHAPTER 3.1: INSTALLING AND CONFIGURING ADD-ONS

Once you have developed your custom add-on for Magento, installing and configuring it is the next step in the process. This step requires special attention, as it directly impacts the success of your add-on. The installation process involves uploading the add-on files to the server and using the Magento Connect Manager to install the add-on. In some cases, manual installation may be required. After installation, configuring the add-on is crucial for its proper functioning. This includes setting up any necessary configurations, updating the database, and ensuring that the add-on is compatible with other installed add-ons. It is important to follow best practices during this step, such as taking a backup of the existing system before installation and carefully reading and understanding the installation and configuration instructions provided with the add-on. Proper installation ensures that your add-on works as expected and provides the desired functionality, improving the overall user experience of your website.

SUBCHAPTER 3.2: TESTING AND TROUBLESHOOTING ADD-ONS

After installation and configuration, testing your add-on is necessary to ensure that it is functioning as expected. This includes testing its compatibility with all existing extensions and recognizing any conflicts and errors that may arise. Thorough testing is crucial as it ensures that all aspects of the add-on are working correctly and prevents the creation of future issues. You can also use online tools like Firebug or WebTools to debug any issues. In case of any issues, troubleshooting comes into play. This involves identifying the cause of any errors and fixing them. This can be done by reviewing the code and checking for any errors, testing different configurations, and seeking support from the add-on provider. To conclude, deploying a custom add-on into the Magento ecosystem requires careful and thorough implementation, testing, and troubleshooting. By following best practices during each of these steps, your add-on can function seamlessly, providing maximum value to users while preventing potential errors and issues.

SUBCHAPTER 3.1: INSTALLING AND CONFIGURING ADD-ONS

The process of installing and configuring add-ons for Magento is relatively straightforward, provided you follow the correct steps. Before installation, you will need to ensure that your store's version is compatible with the add-on you plan to install. Additionally, it is always a good idea to backup your website in case any issues arise during the installation process. Once you have ensured compatibility and backed up your website, the first step is to download the add-on from a reliable source. Many add-ons can be found on Magento's official marketplace, but there are also a variety of third-party sources available. After downloading the add-on, you will need to log in to your Magento admin panel and navigate to the System menu. From there, select the Magento Connect Manager and enter your login credentials. Next, upload the add-on file you downloaded. Once the file has been uploaded, you will need to click on the "Install" button to begin the installation process. Follow the prompts and make any necessary configuration changes, such as enabling or disabling features of the add-on. After installation and configuration, it is important to test the add-on to ensure that it is functioning properly. You may want to perform a variety of tasks, such as placing an order or testing the functionality of the add-on's features. Remember that some add-ons may require additional configuration, such as integration with third-party services or coding changes.

Be sure to carefully follow any installation instructions provided by the add-on developer, and seek assistance from a professional if needed. Installing and configuring add-ons for Magento can be a relatively simple process, but it is important to follow the correct steps and take the necessary precautions to avoid issues. By properly testing and confirming the functionality of any add-ons you install, you can ensure that your store runs smoothly and effectively serves your customers' needs.

TESTING AND TROUBLESHOOTING ADD-ONS

After developing and implementing your custom add-on for Magento, it is essential to test its functionality and effectiveness thoroughly. Testing your add-on will ensure that it doesn't harm the system, and it meets your business objectives. Here are some important testing steps to take:

Functionality Testing

Functionality testing should be at the heart of your testing plan. It involves assessing the functionality of your add-on and ensuring that it accomplishes what it was built to do. During functionality testing, you'll need to confirm that the add-on works as expected, meets user requirements and expectations, and integrates correctly with other systems.

Performance Testing

Performance testing is another crucial aspect of testing your add-on. It addresses the speed, stability, and responsiveness of your add-ons, which can significantly impact the overall experience of your Magento store. Some performance testing elements to consider include load testing, stress testing, and endurance testing.

Security Testing

Security testing is vital to safeguarding the integrity of your Magento store and user data. This testing ensures that the custom add-on does not pose any security risks or vulnerabilities to the Magento store. Security testing involves identifying potential threats, vulnerabilities, and risks, and developing countermeasures to mitigate them.

Troubleshooting

Despite your best efforts, some issues can arise with your add-ons. It is essential to have a system for debugging and resolving these problems. Magento offers various tools to assist in troubleshooting issues, including error logs and a debugging toolbar. Proper troubleshooting techniques will help ensure your add-on is coherent, efficient, and functional. In conclusion, testing and troubleshooting your Magento add-ons are essential for ensuring quality, reliability, and stability. These activities will help you identify and resolve any issues or bugs that may affect the performance of your add-on and ensure it performs optimally.

Chapter 4: Marketing and Selling Add-Ons

Marketing and selling custom add-ons for Magento can be a lucrative business. However, the success of your add-ons depends heavily on how well you market and sell them. In this chapter, we will discuss some strategies you can use to effectively market and sell your custom add-ons.

SUBCHAPTER 4.1: CREATING A MARKETING STRATEGY

Before you can effectively market your custom add-ons, you need to create a marketing strategy. Here are some steps you can follow:

Identify Your Audience

The first step in creating a marketing strategy is to identify your audience. Who needs your add-ons? What problems do they face that your add-ons can solve? Knowing your audience will help you effectively target your marketing efforts.

Create a Unique Selling Proposition

Once you have identified your audience, you need to create a unique selling proposition (USP). Your USP should clearly define what sets your add-ons apart from the competition. What benefits do your add-ons offer that others do not?

Choose Your Marketing Channels

There are many different marketing channels you can use to promote your custom add-ons. Some of the most common channels include: - Social media - Email marketing - Content marketing - Paid advertising - Affiliate marketing Consider which channels are most likely to reach your target audience and create a marketing plan that utilizes those channels.

SUBCHAPTER 4.2: PRICING AND LICENSING ADD-ONS

Pricing and licensing your custom add-ons can be a tricky process. You want to ensure that you are charging a fair price for your add-ons, while also making a profit. Here are some tips to help you price and license your add-ons:

Research Your Competitors

One of the best ways to determine pricing for your custom add-ons is to research your competitors. Look at what they are charging for similar add-ons and use that information to determine what a fair price would be for your add-ons.

Consider a Tiered Pricing Structure

Consider offering a tiered pricing structure for your add-ons. This allows customers to choose a pricing plan that fits their needs.

For example, you could offer a basic plan that includes only the essential features of your add-on, and a premium plan that includes additional features.

Choose the Right Licensing Model

There are several different licensing models you can use for your custom add-ons. Some of the most common include: - Perpetual license: Customers pay a one-time fee for the add-on and can use it indefinitely. - Subscription license: Customers pay a recurring fee to use the add-on. - Freemium license: Customers can use a limited version of the add-on for free, but must pay to access premium features. Consider which licensing model makes the most sense for your add-ons and your target audience.

SUBCHAPTER 4.3: BUILDING A SALES TEAM

Having a sales team can help you effectively market and sell your custom add-ons. Here are some tips for building a successful sales team:

Hire the Right People

When hiring a sales team, it is important to find people who are experienced in sales and have a good understanding of your target audience. Look for individuals who are highly motivated and have a proven track record of success.

Provide Training

Provide your sales team with training to ensure they have a good understanding of your custom add-ons and how they can solve your target audience's problems. This will help them effectively sell your add-ons.

Offer Incentives

Consider offering incentives to your sales team for meeting sales goals. This will help motivate your team to work harder and sell more add-ons. By following these strategies, you can effectively market and sell your custom add-ons for Magento, and increase your revenue.

CREATING A MARKETING STRATEGY

After creating your custom add-ons, it is essential to have a robust marketing strategy to market, promote, and sell them. Without proper marketing, your custom add-ons may not generate the desired revenue, and your efforts may go to waste. Here are some key steps to creating an effective marketing strategy:

Identify Your Target Audience

The first step in creating a marketing strategy is identifying your target audience.

Who are the customers you want to attract? What are their needs and wants? Which channels do they use to find information about products similar to yours? Understanding your target audience helps to tailor your marketing messages to their specific needs.

Create Compelling Messaging

Once you know your target audience, you need to create messaging that speaks directly to them. Your messages should highlight the unique benefits of your custom add-ons over the competition. Use clear and concise language, images, and videos to create compelling messaging that captures the attention of your target audience.

Use Multiple Marketing Channels

To reach your target audience effectively, you need to use multiple marketing channels. Social media, email marketing, content marketing, paid advertising, and attending industry events are all effective ways to promote your custom add-ons. Use a combination of these channels to create a robust and diversified marketing approach.

Pricing Strategy

Your pricing strategy plays a critical role in your marketing efforts. Determine a pricing model that works best for your target audience and your business goals. Will you use a one-time payment model or a subscription-based model? What software licenses or add-ons will you include in your pricing? These factors will impact the overall perceived value of your custom add-ons, which ultimately impacts your marketing efforts.

Define Your Sales Strategy

Lastly, define a sales strategy that supports your marketing efforts. How will you engage with potential customers? Will you use a self-service model or provide personalized sales support? Will you offer free trials or demos? Your sales strategy should support your marketing messaging and make it easy for customers to purchase your custom add-ons and see the benefits firsthand. Creating a successful marketing strategy for your custom add-ons requires time and effort. By following these steps, you can create a marketing approach that engages with your target audience, drives sales, and generates revenue.

PRICING AND LICENSING ADD-ONS

Once you've created your custom add-on for Magento, it's time to think about how to price and license it. These decisions can have a significant impact on your add-on's success in the market, so it's important to give this step the attention it deserves.

Pricing Add-Ons

When deciding on pricing for your add-on, you'll need to consider a few different factors. First and foremost, you need to ensure that your pricing is competitive, taking into account what other similar add-ons are priced at. However, you also need to make sure that you are making a profit on each sale. One of the most common pricing structures for add-ons is a one-time fee, which gives customers access to the add-on indefinitely. Another option is to charge a recurring subscription fee, which ensures a steady stream of income. You should also think about offering different pricing tiers, with more advanced features offered at a higher price point. This allows customers to choose the level of functionality that they need, while still generating revenue for your business.

Licensing Add-Ons

Next, you'll need to determine how you will license your add-on. There are many different licensing models to choose from, so it's important to research each one and choose the one that best fits your business model. One option is a per-user license, which charges customers based on the number of users that will be accessing the add-on. Another option is a site-wide license, which charges a flat fee for unlimited use of the add-on on a single website. It's also important to consider how you will enforce your licensing. You can choose to use a simple key-based system, where a unique license key is generated for each customer. Alternatively, you can opt for more advanced licensing solutions that require periodic license checks to ensure that the add-on is being used appropriately. By carefully considering your pricing and licensing strategy, you can ensure that your add-on is profitable and successful in the market.

BUILDING A SALES TEAM

Creating and selling custom add-ons for Magento can provide a lucrative source of income for your business. However, having a solid sales team in place is essential for success. Here are some tips for building a sales team that can make your product a success:

1. Define roles and responsibilities

Before hiring a sales team, it is essential to define the roles and responsibilities required for your team. This can include identifying the skills and expertise needed for each position, such as sales representatives and account managers. Clear definitions make it easier to identify the right candidates who will fit the job requirements.

2. Hire the right talent

The right sales team can make all the difference in the success of your custom add-ons. Look for candidates who have previous sales experience, exceptional communication skills, and who are capable of working in a fast-paced and competitive environment. We recommend conducting a thorough screening process that includes resume reviews, phone interviews, and in-person interviews.

3. Train your team

Once you have identified and hired the right team members, it's important to provide training to ensure that they understand your products and your sales strategy. Provide training on your product offerings, communication style, and sales techniques, so your team can confidently and effectively sell your custom add-ons.

4. Set clear goals

Set clear goals and targets for your sales team to achieve, and regularly review their progress. You can use tools like Salesforce or HubSpot to set targets, track performance, and monitor progress. By setting clear goals, your team can stay motivated and focused on achieving success.

5. Reward and incentivize your team

Rewarding and incentivizing your sales team can be a powerful motivator. Provide commission or bonuses for hitting sales targets, and recognize individual or team achievements. This can help keep your sales team motivated and focused on achieving success. Building a successful sales team is critical for scaling your custom add-on business. With the right strategy, hiring process, training, and incentives, your sales team can become a key driver for your business's success.

Add-On Maintenance and Support

Once your custom add-ons have been implemented into your Magento store, it is crucial to keep them maintained and provide support to your customers. In this chapter, we will discuss best practices for providing excellent customer service, regular maintenance and updates, and dealing with add-on compatibility issues.

PROVIDING CUSTOMER SUPPORT

Customer support is an essential aspect of maintaining successful custom add-ons. Providing excellent support to your customers creates a loyal customer base, which is essential for the growth and success of your business. To provide the best possible service to your customers, consider implementing a support ticket system. This system provides an organized approach to managing customer inquiries, making it easier for you to respond to queries in a timely and efficient manner. Make sure that your support team is knowledgeable about your custom add-ons and is trained to provide excellent customer service. It is also crucial to establish clear communication with your customers. Make sure that you are transparent about any issues or delays that may arise and are proactive in addressing them. Regularly update your customers about the status of their inquiries and provide them with detailed solutions to any problems they may be experiencing.

REGULAR MAINTENANCE AND UPDATES

Regular maintenance and updates are necessary to ensure the performance and reliability of your custom add-ons. It is essential to schedule regular maintenance to identify and resolve potential issues or vulnerabilities before they impact your customers. Regular updates also ensure that your add-ons are compatible with the latest Magento versions, ensuring that your store functions optimally. When scheduling maintenance and updates, make sure to provide clear communication to your customers about any potential downtime or changes that may affect their experience. Plan maintenance and updates in advance, and provide your customers with ample notice before any scheduled downtime.

DEALING WITH ADD-ON COMPATIBILITY ISSUES

Compatibility issues are an inevitable part of developing custom add-ons for Magento. As Magento frequently updates its core software, certain add-ons may become incompatible with new versions of the platform. To deal with compatibility issues, make sure that you stay up-to-date with the latest Magento releases and plan updates and maintenance accordingly. Regularly test your add-ons against the latest Magento releases to identify any potential conflicts. In the event of compatibility issues, provide proactive communication to your customers and work quickly to resolve any issues. By providing excellent customer support, regular maintenance and updates, and proactive communication with your customers, you can ensure the longevity and success of your custom add-ons on Magento.

PROVIDING CUSTOMER SUPPORT

Once your custom add-ons for Magento are up and running, it's crucial to provide exceptional customer support. This will keep your customers satisfied and increase the likelihood of repeat purchases and positive word-of-mouth. First and foremost, establish clear communication channels for customer support. This can include email, phone, live chat, or a support ticket system. Make sure to respond promptly to all inquiries and provide thorough and helpful solutions to any problems customers may encounter. Additionally, it's important to document common issues and their solutions so that your support team can quickly and efficiently assist customers in the future. This can also be beneficial in identifying recurring issues or areas where improvement is needed in your add-ons. It's also a good idea to have a comprehensive knowledge base or FAQ section on your website for customers to easily find answers to common questions. This reduces the workload on your support team and empowers customers to solve simple problems on their own. Finally, strive to go above and beyond in your customer support efforts. This can include offering personalized solutions, providing additional resources or tutorials, or even just taking the time to check in with customers to ensure they are satisfied with their experience. By providing outstanding customer support, you can build strong relationships with your customers and differentiate yourself from competitors.

SUBCHAPTER 5.2: REGULAR MAINTENANCE AND UPDATES

Regular maintenance and updates are crucial to ensure the smooth running of a Magento store with custom add-ons. It is important to keep the add-ons up-to-date with the latest security patches and bug fixes, as well as ensure compatibility with new versions of Magento. One way to stay on top of maintenance and updates is to establish a schedule for regular check-ins and assessments. This can be done monthly, bi-monthly, or quarterly, depending on the size and complexity of the store and the add-ons involved. During these check-ins, it is important to test the add-ons thoroughly and identify any issues that may have arisen since the last update. When updating add-ons, it is important to follow best practices and ensure that the site is backed up before making any changes. This will ensure that any issues that arise during the update process can be quickly resolved and that data loss is minimized. Additionally, it is important to update the add-ons in the correct order, following any instructions provided by the vendor. Regular maintenance and updates also involve monitoring the performance of the add-ons. This can be done through regular performance testing and monitoring tools.

By keeping a close eye on performance metrics, store owners can quickly identify any issues and address them before they become larger problems. In addition to regular maintenance, it is also important to keep track of any new updates or versions of add-ons. By staying on top of these changes, store owners can ensure that their site is always running the latest, most secure version of the add-ons. This can be done by subscribing to vendor email lists or social media channels and keeping up-to-date with industry news and trends. Overall, regular maintenance and updates are essential to keeping a Magento store with custom add-ons running smoothly. By establishing a schedule for check-ins and assessments, following best practices during updates, and keeping an eye on performance metrics, store owners can ensure that their site is always up-to-date and secure.

DEALING WITH ADD-ON COMPATIBILITY ISSUES

One of the most common challenges faced by developers and merchants alike is ensuring that add-ons are compatible with the Magento platform. This is particularly true in cases where the add-on was developed by a third-party vendor or if it has not been updated in a while. To address these compatibility issues, it is important to follow some best practices. For example, before installing any add-on, it is recommended that you check the version of Magento that the add-on was built for. This information can usually be found in the add-on documentation or in the vendor's website. If the add-on is not compatible with the version of Magento you are using, there are several options available to you. First, you can contact the vendor or developer and request a patch or update that will make the add-on compatible with your version of Magento. Another option is to look for similar add-ons that are compatible with your version of Magento. If you are a developer, it is recommended that you follow Magento's guidelines for add-on development. This will help ensure that your add-ons are always compatible with the latest version of Magento. In addition, regular updates and maintenance of your add-ons can help reduce the risk of compatibility issues. It is also a good idea to test all add-ons before deploying them in a production environment. By taking these steps, you can help ensure that your custom add-ons are always compatible with the Magento platform and that your online store is running smoothly and efficiently.

Chapter 6: Case Studies of Successful Add-On Implementation

In this chapter, we will explore real-life case studies of successful implementation of custom add-ons for Magento. The purpose of this chapter is to showcase various examples of how add-ons can be used to solve specific business needs and to inspire readers to consider using custom add-ons for their own online stores.

SUBCHAPTER 6.1: CASE STUDY 1

One successful implementation of a custom add-on involved the integration of a customer loyalty program into a Magento-based online store. The store owner noticed that their customers often made repeat purchases and wanted to incentivize them to continue doing so. With the help of a development team, they created a custom loyalty program add-on that awarded points to customers for every purchase they made. This add-on allowed customers to redeem their points for discounts on future purchases, creating a win-win situation for both the store owner and the customers. The loyalty program improved customer satisfaction and encouraged repeat purchases, resulting in a significant increase in revenue for the store.

SUBCHAPTER 6.2: CASE STUDY 2

Another successful implementation involved the creation of a custom payment gateway add-on for a Magento-based store that primarily sold products to international customers. The store owner noticed that many of their international customers had difficulty completing their purchases due to limited payment options. With the help of a development team, they created a custom payment gateway add-on that allowed customers to make purchases using a variety of international payment methods. This add-on greatly improved the checkout process for international customers, resulting in a significant increase in sales from this customer segment.

SUBCHAPTER 6.3: CASE STUDY 3

In yet another successful implementation of a custom add-on, a Magento-based online store created a custom shipping module. The store owner noticed that their customers often abandoned their carts due to high shipping costs. With the help of a development team, they created a custom shipping module that calculated shipping costs based on the customer's location, the weight and size of the products, and the shipping method. This module allowed for more accurate shipping cost calculations and greatly improved the checkout process for customers, resulting in a decrease in cart abandonment and an increase in sales. These case studies demonstrate the potential benefits of custom add-ons for Magento-based online stores. By identifying specific business needs and working with a development team, store owners can create custom add-ons that improve customer satisfaction and increase revenue.

CASE STUDY 1

In this case study, we will explore how a custom add-on for Magento was implemented by XYZ Company, resulting in a significant increase in revenue and customer satisfaction. XYZ Company was a large retailer of electronics with an online presence. They wanted to streamline their checkout process and offer customers the ability to checkout with just one click, without compromising on security. They decided to create a custom add-on for their Magento store that would enable one-click checkout while incorporating the necessary security features. To achieve this, XYZ Company hired a team of experienced Magento developers to plan and implement the custom add-on. The team identified the business requirements and created a development plan that incorporated Magento development best practices. The custom add-on was initially tested and optimized locally to ensure compatibility with the existing systems and Magento platform. After testing was complete, the add-on was integrated into the live site and tested rigorously to ensure that it was functioning as intended. The add-on was configured to meet the specific requirements of XYZ Company, with emphasis given to security, ease of use, and simplicity. Upon launch, the custom add-on received positive feedback from customers as it significantly simplified the checkout process while ensuring the highest levels of security. The one-click checkout feature led to a significant increase in conversion rates, resulting in a boost in revenue for XYZ Company. This case study shows how customized add-ons can significantly improve the user experience and revenue for an online store. It also highlights the importance of proper planning, development, testing, and implementation when creating custom add-ons for Magento.

CASE STUDY 2

In this case study, we'll be discussing how a small e-commerce business was able to increase their revenue by implementing custom add-ons for their Magento store. The business, which primarily sold handmade clothing and accessories, was struggling to keep up with the competition in their niche market. They had a small customer base and were struggling to generate enough revenue to sustain the business. After consulting with a Magento developer, they decided to implement several custom add-ons to enhance the user experience on their website and make it easier for customers to find and purchase products. One of the key add-ons they implemented was a custom search filter that allowed customers to sort products by color, size, and other relevant attributes. This made it easier for customers to find the exact product they were looking for, ultimately leading to an increase in sales.

They also implemented a custom discount system that automatically applied discounts to bulk purchases. This encouraged customers to purchase more products, as they knew they would be getting a better deal. Another key add-on was a personalized product recommendation system, which suggested products to customers based on their browsing history and purchase history. This increased the chances of customers finding products they were interested in, ultimately leading to more sales. Overall, these custom add-ons helped the business increase their revenue by 45% within six months of implementation. They were able to better compete in their niche market and continue to grow their customer base as a result.

CASE STUDY 3

In this case study, we will discuss how a clothing retailer was able to significantly increase their revenue by implementing a custom add-on for their Magento store. The retailer was facing a common problem in the e-commerce space - cart abandonment. Despite having a large customer base, they were losing potential sales due to customers abandoning their online shopping carts. After analyzing the data, they identified several reasons for this behavior - lack of payment options, confusing checkout process, and slow page loading speed. To address these issues, the retailer decided to implement a custom add-on that would streamline the checkout process and provide customers with more payment options. The add-on also included automated follow-up emails for customers who abandoned their carts, reminding them of their pending purchase and incentivizing them to complete the transaction. After implementing the custom add-on, the results were immediate. The retailer's cart abandonment rate decreased by 35%, and their overall revenue increased by 20%. The add-on also received positive feedback from customers who appreciated the seamless checkout process and additional payment options. This case study highlights the importance of identifying and addressing customer pain points through custom add-ons. By understanding your customers' needs and implementing solutions that cater to them, you can significantly improve your e-commerce business's revenue and customer satisfaction.

Chapter 7: Future Developments in Custom Add-Ons for Magento

SUBCHAPTER 7.1: EMERGING TRENDS IN E-COMMERCE

E-commerce is constantly evolving, and keeping up with the latest trends is crucial for any business to stay ahead of the competition. Some of the emerging trends that are likely to shape the future of e-commerce include:

1. Mobile commerce

Mobile devices are becoming more powerful and ubiquitous with each passing year, and shoppers are increasingly turning to their smartphones and tablets to make purchases. This means that businesses need to have a mobile-friendly presence, whether that's with a responsive website or a dedicated mobile app.

2. Personalization

Customers expect a personalized shopping experience that caters to their individual needs and preferences. To achieve this, businesses need to collect and analyze customer data, and use that information to tailor their offerings and marketing messages.

3. Augmented reality

Augmented reality (AR) technology allows customers to virtually try on products before they buy, giving them a more immersive and interactive shopping experience. This technology is already being used in the fashion and beauty industries, and is likely to become more widespread in the coming years.

SUBCHAPTER 7.2: MAGENTO COMMUNITY CONTRIBUTIONS

Magento has a vibrant community of developers, designers, and merchants who are constantly working to improve the platform and create new add-ons and extensions. The Magento Marketplace is home to thousands of custom add-ons and themes, many of which are free or low-cost. In addition, the Magento Community Engineering team regularly releases updates and patches to address security issues and bugs, as well as new features and functionality. This open-source approach means that businesses can benefit from the collective knowledge and expertise of the Magento community.

SUBCHAPTER 7.3: THE FUTURE OF CUSTOM ADD-ONS FOR MAGENTO

Custom add-ons will continue to play a crucial role in the success of e-commerce businesses that use Magento. With the platform's flexibility and scalability, there are endless possibilities for creating unique and innovative add-ons that can help businesses stand out in a crowded market. As technology continues to evolve, there will be new opportunities to integrate cutting-edge features and functionality into custom add-ons. For businesses that stay ahead of the curve and embrace these developments, the future of e-commerce looks bright.

EMERGING TRENDS IN E-COMMERCE

E-commerce is an ever-evolving industry that requires businesses to keep up with the latest trends and technologies in order to stay competitive. As consumer behavior and expectations change, it's important for Magento merchants to not only adapt but also to anticipate the future trends. One of the emerging trends in e-commerce is the rise of social shopping. With the growing popularity of social media platforms, more and more consumers are using them to discover new products and make purchases directly within the app. Merchants can take advantage of this trend by integrating their Magento store with social media platforms to provide a seamless shopping experience. Another trend in e-commerce is the use of augmented reality (AR) and virtual reality (VR) technologies. These technologies allow customers to visualize products in a more immersive way, which can increase their confidence in their purchasing decisions. Merchants can leverage AR and VR by implementing product configurators and virtual try-on features on their Magento store. The demand for personalized experiences is also increasing in e-commerce. Customers expect tailored recommendations and suggestions based on their browsing and purchasing history. Magento merchants can provide personalized experiences by implementing machine learning algorithms and data-driven marketing strategies. Finally, another trend in e-commerce is the rise of sustainability and ethical consumerism. Customers are becoming more aware of environmental and social issues and are looking for products that align with their values. Magento merchants can cater to this trend by offering eco-friendly products and implementing sustainable practices in their supply chain. By keeping up with these emerging trends in e-commerce, Magento merchants can stay ahead of the competition and provide their customers with the exceptional shopping experience they expect.

MAGENTO COMMUNITY CONTRIBUTIONS

Magento owes much of its success to its strong community of developers, users, and contributors. The community has played a significant role in shaping and improving Magento over the years. Community contributions have led to the creation of several useful add-ons, modules, and extensions that have helped Magento users achieve their business goals and overcome complex challenges. These community contributions are typically shared through online marketplaces, websites, and forums. Magento's community-driven approach to development has led to the creation of a vast library of open-source code, documentation, and resources. This wealth of information can be accessed by developers, business owners, and users seeking to improve their Magento skills and knowledge. Magento's online community is also a platform for knowledge sharing, idea generation, and problem-solving. Developers can engage with the community to discuss ideas, methods, and best practices for developing custom add-ons. In addition, Magento organizes community-driven events, such as Meet Magento and Magento Live, where developers, business owners, and users come together to share knowledge and discuss industry trends. Overall, Magento's strong community is a testament to the platform's versatility, scalability, and reliability. The contributions from the community have made Magento a better platform, and will continue to do so in the future.